# HOW TO PLAY GOLF FOR BEGINNERS:

## *An Ultimate Step-by-Step Guide Accompanied With Instructions to Master Golf's Rule, Etiquette, Equipments and Proper Technique*

## *BY*

## KEITH BROWN

# Table Of Contents

# Introduction

If you're looking to embark on a journey into the world of golf, "How to Play Golf for Beginners" is the perfect companion to guide you through every step of your golfing adventure. This comprehensive book offers a wealth of knowledge, tips, and practical instructions that will help you develop a solid foundation and gain confidence on the golf course.

Written with the novice golfer in mind, this ultimate step-by-step guide covers all aspects of the game, including the rules, etiquette, equipment, and proper techniques. Whether you are completely new to the sport or have dabbled in it occasionally, this book will provide you with a thorough understanding of the game and set you on the path to becoming a skilled golfer.

The book begins by introducing the fundamental rules and etiquette of golf, emphasizing the importance of respect, integrity, and fair play. It outlines the dos and don'ts of the golf course, from proper attire and behavior to basic course navigation. By familiarizing yourself with these aspects, you'll feel confident and comfortable when stepping onto any golf course.

Furthermore, this guide delves into the essential equipment needed for playing golf. It covers the various types of clubs, golf balls, and other accessories, providing valuable insights on how to choose the right equipment to suit your playing style and ability. Additionally, you'll find tips on how to properly care for and maintain your gear, ensuring its longevity and optimal performance.

The core of the book lies in its detailed breakdown of the golf swing and technique. Step-by-step instructions, accompanied by clear illustrations, will assist you in understanding the correct grip, stance, and posture. You'll learn how to execute different types of swings, from the full swing to chipping and putting, gradually refining your skills as you progress through the chapters.

As you dive deeper into the book, you'll discover valuable practice drills and exercises designed to improve your game. These practical exercises will help you develop consistency, accuracy, and distance control, enabling you to approach each shot with confidence and precision.

"How to Play Golf for Beginners" is not just a book; it's a comprehensive roadmap that will empower you to master the game of golf. Through its engaging and accessible style, it aims to inspire beginners to embrace the challenges and rewards of this remarkable sport. So, grab your clubs, open this book, and embark on an exciting journey toward becoming a confident and skilled golfer.

Happy golfing!

# Chapter 1: The Basics of Golf

## Golf: A Brief Overview

Golf is a popular sport played by millions of people around the world. It is a game that combines skill, strategy, and patience. The objective of golf is simple: to hit a small ball into a series of holes with as few strokes as possible. While it may seem straightforward, golf is a sport that requires a good understanding of its basics and a lot of practice to excel.

**Equipment:** To play golf, you need a few essential pieces of equipment. The most important is a set of golf clubs, which typically includes different types of clubs such as a driver, irons, wedges, and a putter.

Golf balls, tees, and a golf bag to carry your clubs are also necessary. It's essential to choose clubs and balls that are suitable for your skill level and playing style.

**Course and Holes:** Golf is played on a course consisting of 18 holes, although there are also courses with 9 holes. Each hole has a tee box, fairway, rough, and green. The tee box is where you start each hole, and the green is where the hole is located. The fairway is the well-manicured grass area between the tee box and the green, while the rough is the longer grass surrounding the fairway.

**Scoring:** Golf uses a scoring system called stroke play. The objective is to complete each hole using the fewest number of strokes possible. Every time you hit the ball, it counts as one stroke. The score for each hole is the total number of strokes taken to reach the green and then sink the ball into the hole. The player with the lowest total score at the end of the round is the winner.

**Golf Swing:** The golf swing is the fundamental action used to hit the ball. It involves a sequence of movements that require coordination and technique. The swing consists of a backswing, downswing, and follow-through. Proper grip, stance, and alignment are crucial for an effective swing. Developing a consistent and repeatable swing is essential for success in golf.

**Etiquette and Rules:** Golf is known for its strict etiquette and rules. Golfers are expected to follow certain behavior guidelines, such as being quiet and respectful on the course, repairing divots and ball marks, and not disturbing other players. There are also rules governing ball movement, out-of-bounds, hazards, and penalties for rule violations. Familiarizing yourself with these rules is essential to ensure fair play and maintain the integrity of the game.

**Practice and Improvement:** Golf is a sport that requires practice and dedication to improve. Spending time on the driving range, working on your swing, and practicing putting are all essential components of becoming a better golfer. Additionally, playing rounds on the course allows you to apply your skills in a real game scenario and gain experience.

Golf is a challenging yet rewarding sport that offers a combination of physical and mental stimulation. By understanding the basics of golf, including equipment, scoring, swing, etiquette, and rules, you can begin your journey to becoming a proficient golfer. Remember, like any skill, it takes time and effort to improve, so enjoy the process and embrace the challenges that come along the way. Happy golfing!

# The Essential Golf Equipment

Golf is a game that requires skill, strategy, and the right equipment. Whether you're a beginner or a seasoned player, having the essential golf equipment is crucial to your success on the course. In this article, we will explore the basics of golf equipment and the items you need to get started.

**Golf Clubs:** Golf clubs are perhaps the most important pieces of equipment for any golfer. They come in different types and are designed for specific shots. The basic set of golf clubs typically includes a driver, fairway woods, irons, wedges, and a putter. Each club has a different loft angle and length, which affects the distance and trajectory of the ball. It's important to have a variety of clubs in your bag to handle different situations on the course.

**Golf Balls:** Golf balls are another essential item you'll need to play the game. They come in different brands, models, and construction types, all of which can affect the ball's performance. Beginners often opt for two-piece golf balls, which provide distance and durability. As you progress, you may experiment with different types of balls to find the one that suits your playing style.

**Golf Bag:** A golf bag is used to carry and organize your clubs, balls, and other accessories. Golf bags come in various styles, including carry bags, cart bags, and stand bags. Choose one that fits your needs and preferences, considering factors such as weight, storage capacity, and comfort.

**Golf Tees:** Golf tees are small pegs that are used to elevate the ball off the ground for the first shot on each hole. They are typically made of wood or plastic and come in different lengths. The choice of tee depends on the club and the player's preference. Make sure to have a few tees in your bag as they can be easily lost during a round.

**Golf Gloves:** Golf gloves provide grip and control while swinging the club. They are usually made of leather or synthetic materials and are worn on the lead hand (left hand for right-handed players and vice versa). Gloves help prevent blisters and improve the overall feel of the club. It's a good idea to have at least one glove in your bag as a backup.

**Golf Shoes:** Golf shoes are designed to provide stability and traction during the swing. They typically have spikes on the soles to grip the turf. Golf courses often require players to wear soft-spiked shoes to protect the greens. Invest in a comfortable pair of golf shoes that fit well and offer the necessary support for long hours on the course.

**Other Accessories:** There are several other accessories that can enhance your golfing experience. These include a golf hat or visor to protect you from the sun, a golf umbrella for rainy days, a divot repair tool to fix ball marks on the green, and a golf towel to keep your clubs and balls clean. Additionally, a rangefinder or GPS device can help you accurately measure distances on the course.

Remember, while having the right equipment is important, golf is ultimately a game of skill and practice. So, invest in quality equipment that suits your game, but also focus on developing your technique and understanding the nuances of the sport. With time and dedication, you'll be on your way to mastering the game of golf.

# Understanding Golf's Rules and Etiquette

Golf is a popular sport enjoyed by millions of people around the world. Whether you're a beginner or an experienced player, understanding the rules and etiquette of golf is essential for a smooth and enjoyable game. In this article, we'll cover the basics of golf, including the rules and etiquette that govern the sport.

**Rules of Golf:**

**Stroke Play:** In stroke play, each player counts the total number of strokes taken to complete the round. The player with the lowest total score at the end of the round is the winner.

**Match Play:** In match play, players compete against each other hole by hole. The player who wins the most holes wins the match.

**Teeing Off:** Each hole begins with a tee shot. The ball must be placed on or behind the tee markers, and the player must tee off between them. The tee shot is taken from the teeing ground.

**Fairway and Rough:** The fairway is the closely mown area between the tee box and the green. The rough is the longer grass surrounding the fairway. Players should aim to keep their shots on the fairway for better control and distance.

**Hazards:** Hazards include bunkers (sand traps) and water hazards. If your ball lands in a hazard, you may incur a penalty stroke. In some cases, you may have to take a drop outside of the hazard.

**Putting**: On the green, the objective is to putt the ball into the hole. Putts should be rolled along the ground rather than lifted or scooped. The number of putts taken contributes to your overall score.

**Golf Etiquette:**

**Respect the Course:** Take care of the golf course by repairing divots, raking bunkers, and replacing your ball marks on the green. Leave the course as you found it, or preferably in better condition.

**Pace of Play:** Keep up with the group ahead of you to maintain a good pace of play. Be ready to hit when it's your turn, and limit your practice swings and time spent searching for lost balls.

**Silence and Respect:** Golf is a game of concentration, so it's important to remain quiet and still while others are hitting. Avoid unnecessary distractions and be respectful of your fellow players.

**Honesty and Integrity:** Golf is a self-regulated sport, and players are expected to uphold the integrity of the game. Keep an accurate score, follow the rules, and call penalties on yourself when necessary.

**Safety:** Be aware of your surroundings and ensure that it's safe to hit before swinging your club. Never hit your ball if there is a chance of hitting another player or group on the course.

**Dress Code:** Many golf courses have a dress code that requires proper golf attire. Check with the course you're playing at to ensure you're dressed appropriately.

By understanding and following these rules and etiquette guidelines, you'll not only have a better golfing experience but also show respect for the game and your fellow players. Golf is a sport that values tradition, integrity, and good sportsmanship, so embracing these principles will enhance your enjoyment of the game. So, grab your clubs, hit the fairways, and enjoy a round of golf!

# Chapter 2: Mastering the Golf Swing

## Fundamentals of the Golf Swing

Mastering the golf swing is a pursuit that requires dedication, practice, and a solid understanding of the fundamentals. Whether you're a beginner looking to learn the basics or an experienced golfer aiming to refine your technique, focusing on the key elements of the golf swing is essential for achieving consistent and powerful shots. In this article, we will explore the fundamentals of the golf swing and provide valuable insights to help you improve your game.

**Grip:** The grip is the foundation of a successful golf swing. It is crucial to find a grip that feels comfortable and allows for control and flexibility. The most common grips are the overlapping, interlocking, and 10-finger grips. Experiment with different grips and find the one that suits you best.

**Stance and Alignment:** Your stance and alignment play a vital role in setting up a proper swing. Start by positioning your feet shoulder-width apart and aligning them parallel to the target line. Your body should be slightly bent at the waist, and your weight evenly distributed between both feet. Proper alignment ensures that your clubface is square to the target, setting the stage for an accurate shot.

**Posture:** Maintaining good posture throughout your swing is crucial for consistency and power. Stand tall with a straight spine and relaxed shoulders. Bend your knees slightly and tilt your upper body forward. A proper posture allows for a smooth rotation and efficient transfer of energy from your body to the club.

**Backswing:** The backswing sets the stage for a powerful downswing. Start by turning your shoulders away from the target while maintaining a stable lower body. Keep your left arm straight (for right-handed golfers) and allow the club to swing naturally along the intended path. Avoid excessive tension and maintain a smooth tempo.

**Downswing and Impact:** The downswing is where the power is generated. Initiate the downswing by shifting your weight onto your front foot while maintaining a relaxed grip and fluid motion. Rotate your hips and shoulders through the swing, unleashing the stored energy and creating maximum clubhead speed. The moment of impact is crucial, and the clubface should be square to the target for a solid shot.

**Follow-through:** A proper follow-through is a sign of a well-executed swing. After impact, allow your body to continue rotating while extending your arms and club towards the target. The follow-through should be balanced and smooth, demonstrating control and confidence in your swing.

**Practice and Feedback:** Mastering the golf swing takes time and practice. Regularly devote time to the driving range or practice facility to work on your swing mechanics. Experiment with different drills and training aids to refine your technique. Seeking feedback from a golf professional or using video analysis can provide valuable insights into areas of improvement.

Remember, mastering the golf swing is an ongoing process. It requires patience, perseverance, and a willingness to learn and adapt. By focusing on the fundamentals, practicing regularly, and seeking guidance when needed, you can develop a consistent and powerful golf swing that will enhance your enjoyment of the game and lead to improved results on the course. So, grab your clubs, head to the range, and embark on the journey to mastering the golf swing!

# Perfecting Your Grip and Stance

Mastering the golf swing is an essential skill for any golfer looking to improve their game. While there are many elements to a successful swing, two key aspects that require careful attention and practice are the grip and stance. By perfecting these foundational components, golfers can greatly enhance their overall swing and achieve greater accuracy, distance, and consistency on the course.

The grip is the golfer's connection to the club and plays a crucial role in controlling the clubface throughout the swing. A proper grip allows for maximum control and power while minimizing the chances of errant shots. To achieve the correct grip, golfers should start by placing the club in the fingers of their lead hand (the left hand for right-handed golfers) with the clubface square to the target. The grip should feel secure but not overly tight, allowing for a fluid and natural motion during the swing.

Next, the trailing hand (the right hand for right-handed golfers) should be placed on the club, overlapping or interlocking the fingers with the lead hand. Both thumbs should be pointing down the center of the grip, ensuring a unified grip pressure between both hands. It's important to avoid squeezing the club too tightly, as this can hinder wrist movement and lead to tension throughout the swing. Regular practice with the proper grip will help golfers develop muscle memory and a consistent feel for the club.

Equally important to the grip is the golfer's stance, which sets the foundation for a balanced and powerful swing. A good stance promotes proper body alignment and weight distribution, enabling a golfer to generate maximum clubhead speed and maintain stability throughout the swing.

To establish a solid stance, start by positioning the feet shoulder-width apart with the lead foot (left foot for right-handed golfers) flared slightly outward. The weight distribution should be evenly distributed between both feet, with a slight bias toward the lead foot. This helps initiate a proper weight transfer during the swing, allowing for a smooth transition from backswing to downswing.

The posture is also critical in the stance. Golfers should maintain a straight back with a slight bend at the hips, keeping the spine neutral and relaxed. The knees should be flexed, providing stability and balance. It's important to avoid excessive bending or hunching over the ball, as this can restrict the rotation and freedom of movement required for a fluid swing.

Once the grip and stance are established, golfers can focus on developing a consistent and repeatable swing. Regular practice, along with guidance from a golf professional or instructor, can help refine the finer details of the swing and iron out any technical flaws.

mastering the golf swing begins with perfecting the grip and stance. These foundational elements provide the basis for a well-executed swing and allow golfers to achieve greater control, power, and accuracy on the course. By dedicating time and effort to honing these fundamental aspects, golfers can take significant strides towards improving their game and enjoying greater success on the fairways.

# Developing a Consistent Swing Technique

Mastering the golf swing is a pursuit that many golfers embark upon in their quest to improve their game. It is widely recognized that a consistent and effective swing technique is crucial for success on the golf course. Developing a reliable swing not only enhances a golfer's accuracy and distance but also contributes to their overall enjoyment of the sport. In this article, we will explore some key elements to consider when striving to develop a consistent swing technique.

First and foremost, mastering the golf swing requires a solid understanding of the fundamentals. A golfer must familiarize themselves with the basic components of a swing, such as grip, posture, alignment, and ball position. These elements serve as the foundation for a consistent swing and should be thoroughly practiced and ingrained into one's muscle memory. It is essential to seek guidance from a qualified golf instructor or coach who can provide expert advice and help identify any areas for improvement.

One of the most critical aspects of a consistent swing technique is maintaining proper body mechanics throughout the swing. It is crucial to have a smooth and balanced tempo, as well as maintaining good rhythm and timing. Golfers should focus on a full shoulder turn and utilizing their core muscles to generate power. Additionally, maintaining a stable lower body and transferring weight correctly from backswing to downswing is key to achieving consistent ball striking.

Another crucial factor in mastering the golf swing is the development of a repeatable and efficient swing plane. The swing plane refers to the path the clubhead travels during the swing. Ideally, it should follow a consistent and shallow arc, allowing for solid contact and optimal ball flight. Proper swing plane can be achieved through a combination of correct body rotation, arm extension, and clubface control. Regular practice, using video analysis and feedback, can help golfers identify any deviations from the desired swing plane and work towards correcting them.

Furthermore, mastering the golf swing requires a deep understanding of clubface control and impact position. The clubface should be square to the target at impact, with the hands leading the clubhead through the ball. Achieving a proper impact position involves correct wrist hinge, maintaining a flat left wrist (for right-handed golfers), and controlling the clubface angle. Consistent practice and focus on impact position will greatly contribute to a golfer's ability to strike the ball cleanly and with accuracy.

Lastly, mental and physical fitness play a significant role in developing a consistent swing technique. Maintaining a positive mindset, focusing on the present moment, and managing one's emotions are all crucial for executing a consistent swing under pressure. Additionally, incorporating exercises and drills that improve flexibility, strength, and stability will enhance a golfer's physical capabilities and help prevent injuries.

mastering the golf swing and developing a consistent swing technique is a continuous journey that requires dedication, practice, and patience. By focusing on the fundamentals, maintaining proper body mechanics, understanding swing plane and impact position, and prioritizing mental and physical fitness, golfers can significantly improve their swing and overall performance. Remember, seeking guidance from professionals and remaining committed to regular practice are essential for achieving long-term success on the golf course.

# Chapter 3: Essential Golf Shots and Techniques

## Mastering the Tee Shot

In the game of golf, the tee shot is arguably the most crucial shot to master. It sets the tone for the entire hole and can significantly impact a player's overall score. A well-executed tee shot can position the ball favorably for the next shot, while a poorly executed one can lead to trouble and extra strokes. Therefore, understanding and practicing the essential techniques for a successful tee shot is vital for any golfer looking to improve their game.

Here are some key elements to consider when mastering the tee shot:

**Proper Alignment:** Before even addressing the ball, ensuring correct alignment is essential. Position yourself parallel to the target line, with your feet, hips, and shoulders aligned accordingly. This alignment will help you aim accurately and hit the ball towards the desired target.

**Correct Tee Height:** The height at which the ball is teed up can greatly impact the trajectory and distance of the shot. For drivers, the ball should be teed up high, with the top of the ball level with the driver's sweet spot. This setup allows for an upward strike, creating an optimal launch angle. For irons, the ball should be teed slightly lower to promote a more controlled, downward strike.

**Balanced Stance and Grip:** Maintaining a balanced stance is crucial for a consistent tee shot. Distribute your weight evenly between both feet, with a slight tilt towards your front foot. Additionally, grip the club firmly but not too tightly, ensuring a relaxed and fluid swing.

**Controlled Backswing:** During the backswing, focus on maintaining a smooth and controlled motion. Avoid any sudden or jerky movements that can throw off your balance and timing. The backswing should allow you to generate power while maintaining accuracy.

**Effective Downswing and Impact:** The downswing is where the power and accuracy of your tee shot are realized. Start the downswing by shifting your weight from your back foot to your front foot, transferring energy into the ball. Keep your wrists firm, and aim to strike the ball with a slight ascending blow for a higher launch angle and more distance.

**Follow Through:** A proper follow-through is essential for maintaining balance and maximizing the potential of your tee shot. Allow your body to rotate naturally, with your chest facing the target at the end of the swing. A full and controlled follow-through can help ensure a straighter and more accurate shot.

**Practice and Adaptation:** Mastering the tee shot requires consistent practice and adaptation to different course conditions. Spend time on the driving range, focusing specifically on your tee shots. Experiment with different clubs and tee heights to find what works best for you. Additionally, consider the weather, wind conditions, and the layout of the hole to make appropriate adjustments in your approach.

Remember, mastering the tee shot takes time and patience. It's important to practice regularly, seek guidance from golf professionals, and analyze your shots to identify areas for improvement. By honing your tee shot technique, you can gain confidence, enhance your overall game, and enjoy the satisfaction of driving the ball down the fairway with precision and power.

# Navigating Fairway Shots

n the game of golf, mastering fairway shots is crucial for success on the course. These shots occur when you are positioned on the fairway, aiming to hit the ball towards the green. Navigating fairway shots requires a combination of skill, strategy, and proper technique. In this article, we will explore some essential golf shots and techniques to help you improve your fairway play.

## The Approach Shot:

The approach shot is a key fairway shot that allows you to position the ball near the green for a potential birdie or par opportunity. To execute a successful approach shot, it is important to assess the distance to the green and select the appropriate club. Generally, a mid-iron or a hybrid club is preferred for approach shots. Focus on maintaining a smooth swing and striking the ball cleanly, aiming for accuracy rather than distance. Visualize the trajectory and aim to land the ball on the green or in a favorable position for an easy chip or putt.

**The Fairway Wood Shot:**

Fairway wood shots come into play when you need to cover longer distances while maintaining control. These shots are commonly used for reaching the green on a par-5 hole or for hitting longer par-4 holes. When executing a fairway wood shot, select a club with enough loft to generate height and distance. Position the ball slightly forward in your stance, sweep the clubhead through the ball with a smooth, sweeping motion, and maintain balance throughout the swing. Focus on making solid contact and allowing the club to do the work rather than forcing the shot.

**The Layup Shot:**

In certain situations, it may be strategically advantageous to play a layup shot instead of trying to reach the green in one shot. This is especially true when there are hazards, such as water or bunkers, that could lead to a high-risk shot. The layup shot involves intentionally hitting the ball a shorter distance, positioning it in a safe spot on the fairway to set up a more manageable approach to the green. Choose a club that allows you to comfortably clear any hazards and accurately place the ball in the desired landing area. Remember, the goal is to optimize your chances of a good next shot rather than risking a difficult recovery.

**Ball Positioning and Stance:**

Proper ball positioning and stance play a vital role in executing fairway shots effectively. For most fairway shots, position the ball slightly forward of center in your stance to promote a clean strike and a slight upward angle of attack. Keep your feet shoulder-width apart, align your body parallel to the target line, and maintain a relaxed posture. Balancing your weight evenly between both feet helps ensure stability and control throughout the swing.

**Practice and Course Management:**

Lastly, practice and course management are essential aspects of navigating fairway shots successfully. Regularly practice your fairway shots, focusing on different clubs and shot scenarios to develop consistency and confidence. Additionally, familiarize yourself with the layout of the course, including hazards, bunkers, and the location of the green. By studying the course and strategizing your shots accordingly, you can make informed decisions that maximize your chances of success.

Navigating fairway shots in golf requires a combination of skill, strategy, and proper technique. By mastering essential shots like the approach shot, fairway wood shot, and layup shot, and by paying attention to ball positioning, stance, and course management, you can improve your fairway play and lower your scores. Remember, practice and patience are key, and with time, you will enhance your ability to navigate fairway shots with confidence.

# Approaching the Green: Irons and Wedges

When it comes to golf, the ability to approach the green with precision and accuracy is crucial for lowering your scores. The shots you play with irons and wedges are essential for getting the ball close to the hole and giving yourself a good chance for a birdie or par. In this article, we will explore some essential golf shots and techniques for approaching the green using irons and wedges.

**Distance Control:** One of the most important aspects of approaching the green is controlling the distance of your shots. Different irons and wedges have varying degrees of loft, which affects how high and how far the ball will travel. It's crucial to practice and develop a feel for the distance each club can cover. Spend time on the practice range hitting shots with different irons and wedges to understand how far the ball goes with each club.

**Shot Selection:** Golf courses offer a variety of situations and challenges that require different types of shots. For approaching the green, you'll encounter situations such as hitting over water hazards, playing from the rough, or facing a tucked pin placement. Analyze the situation and choose the appropriate club and shot. Sometimes a low-running shot with a mid-iron might be more suitable, while other times a high, soft shot with a wedge is the best option. Assess the conditions and adjust your shot selection accordingly.

**Ball Flight:** Understanding how to control the trajectory of your shots is crucial for approaching the green effectively. Lower trajectory shots are useful when you need to avoid strong winds or when you want the ball to roll more upon landing. On the other hand, higher trajectory shots allow the ball to stop quicker on the greens. To achieve different ball flights, you can adjust your setup, ball position, and swing tempo. Experiment with different techniques to find what works best for you.

**Divot Control:** Proper divot control is essential for consistent and accurate iron and wedge shots. Divots should be taken after impact with the ball, not before. Aim to make divots in front of the ball to ensure solid contact and a descending strike. This ensures that the ball is struck first, compressing it against the clubface and generating the desired ball flight. Practice hitting shots with a focus on taking divots after the ball to improve your divot control.

**Short Game Shots:** Approaching the green with wedges requires proficiency in a variety of short game shots. These shots include pitching, chipping, and bunker shots. When faced with these situations, it's important to have a solid foundation of technique and practice. Develop a consistent and repeatable swing for your short game shots, and practice different distances and lies to improve your versatility around the greens.

Remember, approaching the green with irons and wedges is a skill that takes time and practice to master. Spend dedicated practice sessions honing your distance control, shot selection, ball flight, divot control, and short game shots. Take the time to understand the unique characteristics of each club in your bag and how they can be utilized in different situations. With consistent practice and a focus on these essential golf shots and techniques, you'll be well on your way to improving your scores and enjoying success on the golf course.

# Chapter 4: Mastering the Short Game

## Putting: The Key to Scoring

In the game of golf, few skills are as crucial to scoring well as a solid putting game. While driving the ball long distances may garner applause from the gallery, it is on the greens where championships are won and lost. Putting is often referred to as the "game within the game" due to its significant impact on a golfer's overall score. Therefore, mastering the short game, particularly putting, is essential for any golfer looking to lower their scores and improve their performance on the course.

Putting is both an art and a science. It requires a delicate touch, precise alignment, and a deep understanding of the greens. To become proficient at putting, a golfer must develop a consistent and repeatable stroke that allows for accurate distance control and the ability to read the subtle breaks and slopes on the putting surface.

One of the fundamental principles of putting is alignment. Proper alignment ensures that the golfer's putter face is square to the intended target line, increasing the chances of the ball rolling in the desired direction. Aligning the putter face with the target can be achieved by using various alignment aids or by practicing with visual references on the green, such as intermediate targets or a spot on the back of the ball.

Distance control is another critical aspect of putting. Being able to judge the speed and distance of a putt accurately can be the difference between sinking a birdie or settling for a par. Developing a consistent putting stroke, with a smooth tempo and rhythm, is key to achieving consistent distance control. Practice drills, such as lag putting from various distances, can help golfers refine their feel and touch, leading to improved distance control on the greens.

Reading the greens correctly is perhaps the most challenging skill to master in putting. Understanding the subtle breaks and slopes of the green requires careful observation and experience. Factors such as grass type, grain direction, and terrain can all influence how a putt breaks. Golfers must learn to analyze the green's contours, visualize the ideal path for the ball, and make the necessary adjustments to their aim and stroke. Developing this skill takes time and practice, but it can greatly enhance a golfer's ability to sink putts consistently.

To improve their putting, golfers should incorporate both practice and on-course experience into their training routine. Regular practice sessions on the putting green, focusing on alignment, distance control, and reading greens, can help build confidence and develop the necessary skills. Additionally, playing rounds with a specific emphasis on putting, such as practicing lag putting or attempting to hole every putt within a certain distance, can help golfers simulate real-game situations and improve their performance under pressure.

Mastering the short game, with a particular emphasis on putting, is a key component of scoring well in golf. It requires a combination of technical proficiency, mental focus, and course management skills. By dedicating time and effort to improving their putting game, golfers can enhance their chances of sinking more putts, lowering their scores, and ultimately achieving success on the course. So, grab your putter, head to the practice green, and start honing your skills. The rewards will undoubtedly be seen in your scorecard and your enjoyment of the game.

# Chipping and Pitching: Precision Around the Green

When it comes to the game of golf, one area that often separates the amateurs from the professionals is the short game. Chipping and pitching around the green requires finesse, precision, and a deep understanding of the different shots and techniques involved. Developing these skills can significantly improve your overall golf performance and help you lower your scores. In this article, we will explore the art of mastering the short game, specifically focusing on chipping and pitching.

Chipping and pitching are essential skills for any golfer who wants to improve their game. These shots come into play when you are close to the green and need to get the ball onto the putting surface with accuracy and control. Unlike long drives or fairway shots, chipping and pitching require a delicate touch and a keen sense of distance and trajectory.

Chipping is typically used when you are just off the green, and you want to get the ball rolling along the ground as soon as possible. It involves using a variety of clubs, such as a sand wedge or pitching wedge, to loft the ball onto the green and allow it to roll towards the hole. The key to successful chipping lies in maintaining a consistent and compact swing, keeping your wrists firm, and focusing on the target.

Pitching, on the other hand, is used when you have a slightly longer distance to cover or when there are obstacles, such as bunkers or rough, between you and the green. Pitch shots require more height and spin to stop the ball quickly after it lands on the green. To execute a pitch shot effectively, you need to choose the right club (usually a gap wedge or a lob wedge), create a more substantial backswing, accelerate through the ball, and generate enough loft to achieve the desired trajectory and spin.

**Here are some essential tips to help you master your chipping and pitching skills: Develop a consistent setup:** Position your feet close together, with the ball slightly back in your stance. Lean your weight slightly forward to encourage a descending strike on the ball.

*Control your wrists:* Minimize excessive wrist movement and maintain firmness in your wrists throughout the swing. This will help ensure better contact and consistency in your shots.

**Practice distance control:** Spend time on the practice green, experimenting with different clubs and swings to get a feel for how far the ball will travel with each. Develop a range of shots for various distances and learn to gauge the required force.

**Focus on the landing spot:** Instead of fixating on the hole, pick a specific landing spot on the green and aim for it. This approach will help you control your trajectory and distance more effectively.

**Develop a repeatable swing:** Consistency is crucial in chipping and pitching. Work on developing a repeatable swing motion that you can rely on, regardless of the situation.

**Utilize different clubs:** Experiment with different clubs and understand their characteristics. Learn to adapt your technique and club selection based on the lie, distance, and obstacles around the green.

**Practice under different conditions:** Play with varying slopes, grass lengths, and lies to simulate real-game scenarios. This practice will enhance your ability to adapt to different situations on the course.

**Get comfortable with different shot types:** Master various shot types, including bump-and-run shots, flop shots, and lob shots. Understanding when to use each type and having the confidence to execute them will make you a more versatile player.

Remember, mastering the short game is an ongoing process that requires time, practice, and patience. By dedicating focused practice sessions to chipping and pitching, you can gain confidence and consistency in these essential aspects of your golf game. The ability to navigate the delicate shots around the green with precision will undoubtedly have a positive impact on your overall performance and contribute to lower scores on the course.

# Bunker Shots: Escaping the Sand Traps

Mastering the short game in golf is essential for any golfer looking to improve their overall performance on the course. One crucial aspect of the short game is the ability to escape sand traps or bunkers effectively. Bunker shots can be quite intimidating, but with the right technique and practice, golfers can confidently navigate these hazards and save valuable strokes.

To begin mastering bunker shots, it's important to understand the basic principles behind them. Unlike shots from the fairway or rough, bunker shots require a different approach due to the nature of the sand. The goal is not to strike the ball directly but rather to use the sand as a cushion and propel the ball out of the bunker with the momentum generated.

**Here are some key tips for escaping sand traps and improving your bunker shots:**

**Choose the right club:** Typically, a sand wedge is the most suitable club for bunker shots due to its design, which features a higher bounce angle and wider sole. The bounce of the club helps the clubhead glide through the sand smoothly, preventing it from digging too deeply.

**Set up with an open stance:** Position your feet slightly wider than shoulder-width apart, with your front foot pulled back slightly. This open stance allows you to swing along the intended target line and provides better access to the sand beneath the ball.

**Open the clubface:** Rotate the clubface open by turning the handle of the club slightly towards the target. This open clubface helps create loft and allows the club to glide through the sand effortlessly.

**Aim to hit the sand, not the ball:** Unlike other shots, the goal in a bunker shot is to strike the sand a few inches behind the ball. Aim to create a shallow divot by focusing on the spot where you want the club to enter the sand. Hitting the sand first creates the necessary explosion effect to propel the ball out of the bunker.

**Maintain a consistent tempo:** It's crucial to maintain a smooth and controlled swing throughout the shot. Avoid decelerating or rushing the swing, as this can lead to inconsistent results. Practice a rhythmic swing that allows you to make clean contact with the sand.

**Follow through with the swing:** Complete your swing by allowing the club to follow through after striking the sand. This follow-through helps generate the necessary power and ensures a smooth transition from the sand to the green.

**Practice regularly:** Bunker shots require practice to develop confidence and consistency. Set aside dedicated practice sessions to work on your technique.

Experiment with different lies, distances, and green conditions to simulate real-game scenarios.

Remember, mastering bunker shots takes time and patience. It's essential to remain focused and maintain a positive mindset. Overcoming the fear or apprehension associated with bunkers is crucial to becoming a more well-rounded golfer.

In addition to practicing the physical aspects of bunker shots, mental preparation is also vital. Visualize successful shots, trust your technique, and maintain a calm and composed state of mind when facing bunker challenges on the course.

By dedicating time to mastering the short game and specifically working on bunker shots, golfers can greatly enhance their ability to escape sand traps and improve their overall performance. With practice, patience, and the right technique, the intimidation factor of bunkers can be minimized, allowing golfers to approach these hazards with confidence and save valuable strokes on their way to lower scores.

# Chapter 5: Golf Strategies and Course Management

## Understanding Course Layout and Strategy

Golf is a game that requires not only technical skill but also strategic thinking. While swinging the club and hitting the ball accurately are important, having a solid course management strategy can greatly enhance your chances of success on the golf course. In this article, we will explore the importance of understanding course layout and delve into effective golf strategies and course management techniques.

One of the first steps in developing a successful golf strategy is familiarizing yourself with the course layout. Take the time to study the course's yardage, hazards, and the position of the fairways, bunkers, and water hazards. This knowledge will enable you to plan your shots accordingly, making strategic decisions that maximize your chances of avoiding trouble spots and achieving optimal positioning.

Another essential aspect of course management is considering the strengths and weaknesses of your own game. Assess your driving distance, accuracy, iron play, and short game proficiency. By understanding your own abilities, you can tailor your strategy to play to your strengths while minimizing the impact of your weaknesses. For example, if your driving accuracy is not your strong suit, it may be wiser to use a fairway wood or hybrid off the tee instead of a driver to ensure better placement for your next shot.

Strategic shot selection is a critical component of effective course management. Instead of always going for the longest shot possible, consider the risks involved and the potential rewards. Sometimes, a conservative approach can be more advantageous, especially when facing difficult hazards or narrow fairways. By carefully selecting your shots, you can increase your chances of hitting the fairway, avoiding penalties, and setting up easier approach shots.

Course conditions, including wind direction and speed, should also be factored into your strategy. A strong headwind may require adjustments to your club selection and shot trajectory, while a tailwind can provide an opportunity for extra distance. Paying attention to weather conditions and adapting your strategy accordingly can give you an edge over your competitors.

Furthermore, course management involves having a plan for each hole. Analyze the hole's layout and identify the best landing areas for your shots. Consider where the trouble spots are and determine the safest and most effective route to the green. This level of premeditation can help you avoid unnecessary risks and guide your shot execution throughout the round.

Additionally, it's important to maintain a positive mindset and remain patient on the golf course. Even with a well-crafted strategy, things may not always go according to plan. Stay focused on the present shot and avoid dwelling on past mistakes. Adjust your strategy if necessary, and trust in your abilities to recover from difficult situations.

Finally, regular practice and experience are crucial for developing effective golf strategies and improving course management skills. Spend time practicing different shots and scenarios, both on the driving range and on the course itself. The more you expose yourself to varying course conditions and challenges, the better equipped you'll be to make informed decisions and execute your shots with confidence.

Understanding course layout and developing a thoughtful golf strategy are fundamental aspects of successful course management. By studying the course, considering your own abilities, making strategic shot selections, adapting to course conditions, and maintaining a positive mindset, you can optimize your performance and increase your chances of achieving your golfing goals. Remember, a well-executed game plan can make all the difference in the highly strategic and rewarding game of golf.

# Dealing with Different Course Conditions

Golf is a sport that challenges players to adapt to varying course conditions. From wind and rain to firm or soft fairways, each course presents unique challenges that require careful consideration and strategic decision-making. Developing effective golf strategies and implementing proper course management techniques can greatly enhance a player's performance in different conditions. Let's explore some key strategies for dealing with various course conditions.

## Windy Conditions:

Windy conditions can significantly impact the trajectory and distance of your shots. To tackle the wind effectively, consider the following strategies:

**Adjust your club selection:** Choose a club that will help you keep the ball low and minimize the effect of the wind. For instance, opt for a lower lofted club and play the ball back in your stance.

**Aim accordingly:** Account for the wind's direction and strength when aiming. Aim upwind to allow the wind to push the ball back toward your target.

**Swing adjustments:** Make slight adjustments to your swing, such as swinging more smoothly and keeping the ball flight lower, to counteract the wind's influence.

**Wet Conditions:**

Playing on a wet course demands adjustments to your game to maintain control and prevent excessive spin. Here are some strategies to employ in wet conditions:

**Tee shots:** Use tees that elevate the ball, minimizing contact with wet ground and reducing the chances of losing distance.

**Club selection:** Consider using clubs with more loft, as they generate more backspin and can help prevent shots from skidding or bouncing uncontrollably on wet fairways.

**Short game:** Modify your approach to chip and pitch shots. Opt for higher-lofted wedges and focus on a steeper angle of attack to avoid digging into the wet turf.

**Firm and Fast Conditions:**

On courses with firm and fast conditions, the ball tends to roll out more after landing.

Employ these strategies to optimize your performance:

**Tee shots:** Utilize clubs with lower loft to achieve a lower ball flight and maximize roll-out distance.

**Approach shots:** Adjust your club selection, opting for less loft, to take advantage of the ground's firmness. Aim for the front of the green, allowing the ball to roll toward the hole.

**Putting:** Pay close attention to the speed and slope of the greens. Play with a lighter touch, as the ball will roll out more quickly on firm surfaces.

**Hilly or Undulating Courses:**

Hilly or undulating courses require careful planning and strategic decision-making. Consider the following strategies:

**Club selection:** Take into account the elevation changes and select clubs that will help you clear hazards or reach the intended landing areas.

**Reading the terrain:** Analyze the contours of the fairways and greens to identify the best lines of play. Understand how slopes will affect the direction and speed of your shots.

Smart positioning: Position yourself strategically to have a better angle for the next shot. This might mean playing to the wider side of a fairway or avoiding certain pin positions that are guarded by slopes.

adapting to different course conditions is an essential aspect of golf. By employing effective strategies and implementing proper course management techniques, golfers can navigate through challenging conditions more efficiently. Remember to analyze the situation, make the necessary adjustments in club selection and swing technique, and approach each shot with a thoughtful mindset. With practice and experience, you'll be better equipped to handle any course conditions that come your way.

# Mental Game: Staying Focused and Managing Pressure

In the game of golf, having a strong mental game is just as important as having a solid swing. Staying focused and managing pressure on the course can greatly improve your overall performance and help you achieve better results. Here are some strategies for enhancing your mental game in golf.

**Pre-shot Routine:** Developing a consistent pre-shot routine can help you stay focused and eliminate distractions. This routine could include visualizing the shot, taking practice swings, and aligning yourself with the target. By following the same routine before each shot, you create a sense of familiarity and confidence.

**One Shot at a Time:** Golf is a game that requires patience and a focus on the present moment. Instead of dwelling on past mistakes or worrying about future shots, concentrate on the shot at hand. By adopting a "one shot at a time" mindset, you can channel your energy into executing each shot to the best of your ability.

**Positive Self-Talk:** The way you speak to yourself on the course can have a significant impact on your performance. Use positive self-talk to reinforce confidence and maintain a positive mindset. Instead of dwelling on negative thoughts or mistakes, focus on the opportunities and strengths in your game.

**Breathing and Relaxation Techniques:** When faced with pressure situations, it's important to stay calm and composed. Practice deep breathing exercises or relaxation techniques to manage stress and stay in control. By taking deep breaths and consciously relaxing your muscles, you can reduce tension and make better decisions on the course.

**Visualize Success:** Visualization is a powerful tool in golf. Before each shot, visualize the desired outcome and see yourself executing the shot perfectly. Imagine the ball soaring through the air and landing exactly where you want it to. This mental imagery helps build confidence and prepares your mind and body for success.

**Course Management:** Effective course management involves making smart decisions that maximize your strengths and minimize risks. It's crucial to assess the layout of the course, consider the conditions, and plan your shots accordingly. This includes selecting the right club, playing to your strengths, and avoiding unnecessary hazards.

**Stick to Your Game Plan:** Once you've developed a game plan for the course, stick to it. Avoid getting swayed by the performance of others or taking unnecessary risks. By staying disciplined and following your strategy, you increase your chances of success and maintain a clear focus on your own game.

**Embrace Challenges:** Golf is a challenging sport, and every round presents its own set of obstacles. Rather than getting discouraged by difficult shots or unfavorable conditions, view them as opportunities to showcase your skills and problem-solving abilities. Embracing challenges with a positive mindset can lead to personal growth and improved performance.

Remember, golf is as much a mental game as it is a physical one. By incorporating these strategies into your approach, you can enhance your mental game, stay focused, and effectively manage pressure on the golf course. With practice and persistence, you'll find yourself making better decisions, executing shots with confidence, and ultimately improving your overall performance.

# Conclusion

In conclusion, "How to Play Golf for Beginners: An Ultimate Step-by-Step Guide Accompanied With Instructions to Master Golf's Rules, Etiquette, Equipment, and Proper Technique" serves as a comprehensive resource for aspiring golfers who are eager to embark on their golfing journey. Throughout this book, readers have been introduced to the fundamental aspects of the game, from understanding the rules and etiquette to acquiring the necessary equipment and honing proper techniques.

By following the step-by-step instructions provided within these pages, beginners have gained a solid foundation that will enable them to approach the golf course with confidence and enthusiasm. The book has emphasized the importance of patience, practice, and perseverance, recognizing that mastery of golf is a continuous learning process.

Moreover, the inclusion of detailed explanations, illustrative diagrams, and practical tips has enhanced the reader's understanding and facilitated the application of concepts. This holistic approach ensures that beginners not only grasp the technical aspects of the game but also appreciate the mental and strategic elements that are inherent to golf.

Furthermore, the emphasis on golf etiquette has instilled in readers a sense of respect for the game, fellow players, and the golf course itself. By embracing the etiquette guidelines presented in this book, beginners will not only enhance their own golfing experience but also contribute to a welcoming and harmonious golfing community.

In summary, "How to Play Golf for Beginners" is an invaluable guide that equips novice golfers with the knowledge, skills, and mindset required to navigate the world of golf. Whether it is understanding the rules, selecting the right equipment, or perfecting technique, this book has laid a strong foundation for beginners to build upon as they continue their golfing journey. By immersing themselves in the wisdom and insights shared within these pages, beginners can confidently step onto the course, knowing they possess the tools to enjoy and excel in the game of golf.

Made in the USA
Las Vegas, NV
12 July 2024

92193384R00056